"BRING THE CLASSICS TO LIFE"

REBECCA
OF SUNNYBROOK FARM

LEVEL 1

Series Designer
Philip J. Solimene

Editor
Kathryn L. Brennan

EDCON

Story Adaptor
Laura Machynski

Author
Kate Douglas Wiggin

About the Author

Kate Douglas Wiggin was an American writer and educator. She was born on September 28, 1856 as Kate Douglas Smith in Philadelphia, Pennsylvania. Kate went to a private school in Andover, Massachusetts. She was always interested in education. In San Francisco in 1878, she started the first free kindergarten on the West Coast. Two years later, with her sister Nora, she started the California Kindergarten Training School for teachers. Together with her sister, Mrs. Wiggin prepared many textbooks. She also wrote several other books for children. They include "The Birds' Christmas Carol," "Timothy's Quest," and "Mother Carey's Chickens." Kate died in Harrow, England on August 24, 1923.

Copyright © 1993
A/V Concepts Corp.
Long Island, New York

Printed in U.S.A.
ISBN# 1-55576-046-5

CONTENTS

WORDS USED

Story 11	Story 12	Story 13	Story 14	Story 15
KEY WORDS				
clean	barn	always	anything	both
farm	flowers	angry	let	going
fine	leave	nice	listen	lamp
horse	miss	than	shoe	outside
name	thought	wish	stay	take
NECESSARY WORDS				
money	kiss	cloth	children	again
stagecoach	teacher	dress	Friday	company
	thirsty	errand	mind	idea
	water pail	pink	sneak	soap
		sew	soon	Thanksgiving

WORDS USED

Story 16	Story 17	Story 18	Story 19	Story 20
KEY WORDS				
alike	game	an	any	act
around	herself	garden	most	ago
brother	lazy	hurry	six	does
felt	maybe	sky	soft	grand
milk	never	you're	why	sorry
NECESSARY WORDS				
proud	cane	move	change	dream
	married	parade	letter	mine
visit	newspaper	prize	life	right
	private	stroke	just	wait
	save	watch	railroad	while
	writer/writing		thank	

REBECCA LEAVES THE FARM

PREPARATION

Key Words

clean	(klēn)	free from dirt. *She kept herself <u>clean</u> and neat.*
farm	(färm)	land where food and animals are grown to eat or sell. *Mary feeds the ducks on the <u>farm</u>.*
fine	(fīn)	very nice; best *Mary wore her <u>fine</u> hat to the city.*
horse	(hôrs)	a large four-legged animal with hoofs and tail of long, coarse hair. *Mary's <u>horse</u> runs very fast.*
name	(nām)	word or words that you call someone or something. *Her first <u>name</u> is Jane.*

REBECCA LEAVES THE FARM

Necessary Words

money   (mun´ē)   Coins or paper notes used to buy or sell.
I could not buy anything at the candy store because I left my <u>money</u> home.

stagecoach   (stāj´kōch)   A closed carriage pulled by horses that takes people from one place to another.
My grandfather once rode in a <u>stagecoach</u>.

People

Jeremiah Cobb   The man who drives the stagecoach.

Rebecca Randall   A farm girl who goes to live with her aunts, Miranda and Jane Sawyer.

Places

Riverboro   The town where Aunt Miranda and Aunt Jane live.

school   A place for teaching and learning.

Sunnybrook Farm   The place where Rebecca lives with her family.

REBECCA LEAVES THE FARM

Rebecca tells Jeremiah that she would like to sit up front with him, not inside the coach.
That way, she could see more.

Preview:	1. Read the name of the story.
	2. Look at the picture.
	3. Read the sentences under the picture.
	4. Read the first two paragraphs of the story.
	5. Then answer the following question.

You learned from your preview that
___ a. Rebecca owns a horse.
___ b. Rebecca is leaving her home.
___ c. Rebecca is afraid.
___ d. Rebecca doesn't want any friends.

Turn to the Comprehension Check on page 10 for the right answer.

Now read the story.

Read to find out where Rebecca is going.

REBECCA LEAVES THE FARM

Rebecca Randall had put on her fine, spring coat. That made her happy. She liked fine things. Her mother said she could put it on for her ride to her new home.

She was not afraid to go away from the farm. Her good, old Sunnybrook Farm. She was sure to make new friends.

Rebecca saw the horses come over the hill. The stagecoach (stāj´ kōch) stopped.

"Is this the coach to Riverboro?" Mrs. Randall said to the man.

"Yes," said the man. "My name is Jeremiah Cobb. My horses and I are going to Riverboro."

"Good," said Mrs. Randall. "I want you to take Rebecca to my sisters' house. Sawyer is the name. Miranda and Jane Sawyer."

Mr. Cobb helped Rebecca into the coach.

"I'll be fine, Mother," said Rebecca. "I'll be a good girl and I'll keep my face clean."

The ride to Riverboro was fun, but Rebecca wanted to sit with Jeremiah. He stopped the coach and helped her out. She sat with him the rest of the way.

"My name is Rebecca Randall," she said. "I live on a farm. I will go to school in Riverboro. I will make a lot of money one day. Then I can help with the farm. Father is not living. Mother needs more money for there are so many of us at home."

Mr. Cobb liked Rebecca. She was only ten years old. She was so much fun! And old for her years.

They had come to the Sawyer home. Mr. Cobb helped Rebecca into the house. It was a fine, clean house.

"It's good to see you Rebecca," said Aunt Miranda.

"It's good to see you too," said Rebecca. She looked at Mr. Cobb.

"It was good to ride with you," said Rebecca.

"It was fun for me too," said Jeremiah.

REBECCA LEAVES THE FARM

COMPREHENSION CHECK

Choose the best answer.

1. In the beginning of the story, we find out that Rebecca
___a. does not like people.
___b. is afraid of everything.
___c. owns a horse.
___d. likes fine things.

2. How did Rebecca get from Sunnybrook Farm to Riverboro?
___a. By plane
___b. By stagecoach
___c. By bus
___d. By car

3. What was the stagecoach driver's name?
___a. Jeremiah Cobb
___b. Sam Randall
___c. Miranda Sawyer
___d. Jane Sawyer

4. Rebecca was going to live with
___a. Jeremiah Cobb.
___b. her new friends.
___c. her aunts Miranda and Jane.
___d. her father.

5. Rebecca tells Mr. Cobb that some day she will
___a. run away.
___b. drive a coach.
___c. own a horse.
___d. make a lot of money.

6. Mr. Cobb learns from Rebecca that
___a. her father is not living and her mother needs money.
___b. Sunnybrook Farm burned down.
___c. Aunt Miranda needs money.
___d. she is an only child.

7. Rebecca was going to live with her aunts because
___a. they needed Rebecca's help.
___b. she would be going to school in Riverboro.
___c. Rebecca didn't like her mother.
___d. Rebecca didn't have any other place to live.

8. How do you think Sunnybrook Farm got its name?
___a. The sun always shines there.
___b. The farm is very large.
___c. There is a brook near it and when the sun is on the brook, it shines.
___d. Rebecca was always happy on the farm.

9. Another name for this story could be
___a. "A New Home."
___b. "Don't Cry."
___c. "Run Away Rebecca."
___d. "How To Drive A Stagecoach."

10. This story is mainly about
___a. Rebecca's brothers and sisters.
___b. Rebecca's aunts.
___c. Mr. Cobb's family.
___d. a new life for a young girl.

Check your answers with the key on page 67.

REBECCA LEAVES THE FARM

VOCABULARY CHECK

clean	farm	fine	horse	name

I.   Sentences to Finish

Fill in the blank in each sentence with the correct key word from the box above.

1. I asked the new girl, "What is your _____?"

2. I must _____ my room before I can go out to play.

3. Mother said she would buy me a _____ dress for the party.

4. We went to the _____ to see the pigs.

5. The _____ pulled the big wagon.

II.   Matching

Write the letter of the correct meaning from Column B next to the key word in Column A.

Column A

___ 1. horse

___ 2. name

___ 3. clean

___ 4. farm

___ 5. fine

Column B

a. not dirty

b. land where food is grown to sell

c. it has four legs and a long tail of coarse hair

d. very nice

e. a word that you use to call someone

Check your answers with the key on page 69.

REBECCA GOES TO SCHOOL

PREPARATION

Key Words

barn	(bärn)	a place to keep hay, cows, or horses *John put the horse in the <u>barn</u>.*
flowers	(flou´ərs)	parts of a plant or tree which make the seeds; blossoms *Mary will water the <u>flowers</u>.*
leave	(lēv)	go away; go away from *We will <u>leave</u> the house now.*
miss	(mis)	to feel bad about someone or something gone *Jane did <u>miss</u> her mother.*
thought	(thôt)	idea; thinking *John <u>thought</u> he was a good boy.*

REBECCA GOES TO SCHOOL

Necessary Words

kiss (kis) to touch with the lips as a sign of love
A light <u>kiss</u> touched my face.

teacher (tē´ chər) one who helps you learn in school
Our <u>teacher</u> read us a story.

thirsty (ther´ stē) without water; having nothing to drink; dry
Running makes you <u>thirsty</u>.

water pail (wô tər pāl) a pail filled with water for drinking
Before there was running water, one used to get a drink from a <u>water pail</u>.

People

Miss Dearborn Rebecca's school teacher in Riverboro.

Emma Jane Perkins Rebecca's best friend.

Seesaw Simpson Also named Samuel. One of the many Simpson children.

REBECCA GOES TO SCHOOL

Rebecca just couldn't get enough water. She made many trips to the water pail.

Preview: 1. Read the name of the story.
2. Look at the picture.
3. Read the sentences under the picture.
4. Read the first two paragraphs of the story.
5. Then answer the following question.

You learned from your preview that Miss Dearborn was not happy to see
___ a. Rebecca in school.
___ b. Seesaw Simpson in school.
___ c. Rebecca leave her seat so many times.
___ d. Emma Jane Perkins.

Turn to the Comprehension Check on page 16 for the right answer.

Now read the story.

Read to find out about Rebecca's first day at school.

REBECCA GOES TO SCHOOL

Rebecca made many new friends. Her good friend, Emma Jane Perkins, walked with her to school. They had to walk over a hill by the Simpson barn to get there. Rebecca loved this walk. She thought the flowers on the way were the best she had ever seen.

Her first day in school was a bad one. Rebecca ate fish that morning. She was very thirsty. The teacher, Miss Dearborn, did not like to see her leave her seat. She had gone to the water pail too many times.

Seesaw Simpson was getting thirsty. He would leave his seat when Rebecca would sit down.

"Something funny is going on," thought Miss Dearborn.

"Rebecca," said Miss Dearborn, "go to the water pail. Do not sit until I tell you to," she said.

Rebecca did not make a sound. She went to the water pail. Her face got very red. The boys and girls had laughed.

"I do not like this place," thought Rebecca. "I will leave. I will miss the walks by the Simpson barn, and I will miss the flowers, but I will not miss this school!"

When school was over, Miss Dearborn had Rebecca stay to read from her school book. Rebecca was not happy. Miss Dearborn saw that Rebecca's eyes were wet. But Rebecca read her book out loud:

"If I had not,
If you had not,
If he had not,"

"That is very good, Rebecca," said Miss Dearborn. "Give me one more, and you may go home."

"If I did not love fish," said Rebecca, "I would not have been thirsty."

"And if you had loved this school," said Miss Dearborn, "you did not show it. You were at the water pail all day."

Then Miss Dearborn kissed Rebecca. For she liked her very much.

Rebecca laughed. She had made one more friend.

REBECCA GOES TO SCHOOL

COMPREHENSION CHECK

Choose the best answer.

1. Rebecca loved to walk by the Simpson barn because
   ___a. she thought the flowers along the way were beautiful.
   ___b. it was a short-cut.
   ___c. the candy store was along the way.
   ___d. she liked Seesaw Simpson.

2. Rebecca had to go to the water pail many times because
   ___a. she had to clean it.
   ___b. she had eaten fish for breakfast and was very thirsty.
   ___c. she had to fill it up.
   ___d. there was a fire in the school.

3. Miss Dearborn made Rebecca
   ___a. wash the water pail.
   ___b. get more water.
   ___c. take the water pail outside.
   ___d. stand by the water pail the rest of the day.

4. When Rebecca was sent to stand by the water pail,
   ___a. she ran out of the room.
   ___b. her face got all red.
   ___c. she started to cry.
   ___d. she told Miss Dearborn she hated her.

5. Miss Dearborn thought that Rebecca
   ___a. did not love school.
   ___b. was being silly.
   ___c. was being a baby.
   ___d. was trying to be a class clown.

6. After school, Miss Dearborn
   ___a. called Aunt Miranda.
   ___b. went to see Aunt Jane.
   ___c. told Rebecca to stay and read to her.
   ___d. **told Rebecca she was not to come back to school, ever.**

7. At first, Rebecca thought that Miss Dearborn
   ___a. was very pretty.
   ___b. didn't like her.
   ___c. was very funny.
   ___d. didn't want to teach the children.

8. Rebecca was happy when Miss Dearborn kissed her because
   ___a. no one liked her.
   ___b. Rebecca was all alone.
   ___c. it meant they were friends now.
   ___d. Rebecca's mom never kissed her.

9. Another name for this story could be
   ___a. "A Bad Day at School."
   ___b. "No Good News."
   ___c. "Home Again."
   ___d. "Good-By Again."

10. This story is mainly about
   ___a. Seesaw Simpson's barn.
   ___b. Emma Jane Perkins.
   ___c. how to build a water pail.
   ___d. Rebecca's day at school.

Check your answers with with key on page 67.

REBECCA GOES TO SCHOOL

VOCABULARY CHECK

barn	flowers	leave	miss	thought

I. Sentences to Finish

Fill in the blank in each sentence with the correct key word from the box above.

1. I will _____ you when you are gone.

2. Please go away and _____ me alone.

3. We want to paint the _____ red.

4. Mom was so happy when we gave her _____ that she almost started to cry.

5. I _____ I was going to have a surprise party.

II. Word Use

Put a check next to YES if the sentence makes sense. Put a check next to NO if the sentence does not make sense.

1. Because you are with me, I will <u>miss</u> you.   __ YES __ NO

2. Please come back and <u>leave</u> me.   __ YES __ NO

3. A <u>barn</u> is a place where fish live.   __ YES __ NO

4. I <u>thought</u> that no one was home.   __ YES __ NO

5. Jane placed the cut <u>flowers</u> on the table.   __ YES __ NO

Check your answers with the key on page 69.

AUNT JANE BRINGS SUNSHINE

PREPARATION

Key Words

always	(ôl′ wāz)	at all times; all the time *Mother is always happy.*
angry	(ang′ grē)	feeling or showing anger; to be mad *I was very angry that you hit my dog.*
nice	(nīs)	pleasing; very fine *You have a very nice house.*
than	(T͟Han)	compared to: *John is taller than his sister.* *Jane can read better than John.*
wish	(wish)	to hope for; to want *I wish I had money to buy that doll.*

AUNT JANE BRINGS SUNSHINE

Necessary Words

cloth	(klôth)	a material made from wool, cotton, or silk, etc. *I need some <u>cloth</u> to make a dress.*
dress	(dres)	an item made of cloth worn by women or girls *The little girl was so happy with her new <u>dress</u>.*
errand	(er′ ənd)	a trip to do something *I had an <u>errand</u> to do this morning before coming to school.*
pink	(pingk)	the color you get when you mix red and white; a light or pale red *Those <u>pink</u> flowers are so pretty.*
sew	(sō)	work with a needle and thread; to bring together with stitches *Mom is going to teach us all how to <u>sew</u>.*

People

Hannah	Rebecca's sister who lives back on the farm with the rest of Rebecca's family.
Lorenzo de Medici Randall	Rebecca's father's name.

AUNT JANE BRINGS SUNSHINE

*Every day after school, while Emma Jane and the Simpson children were playing,
Rebecca would have to work on her brown cloth.*

Preview: 1. Read the name of the story.
2. Look at the picture.
3. Read the sentence under the picture.
4. Read the first two paragraphs of the story.
5. Then answer the following question.

You learned from your preview that Rebecca thought
___ a. Aunt Miranda liked her very much.
___ b. Aunt Miranda had wanted Hannah to come, not Rebecca.
___ c. Aunt Miranda like to sew.
___ d. Aunt Jane did not like her.

Turn to the Comprehension Check on page 22 for the right answer.

Now read the story.

Read to find out more about Aunt Miranda and Rebecca.

AUNT JANE BRINGS SUNSHINE

Rebecca did not know how to sew. Aunt Jane showed her how.

"My sister Hannah can do so many things," thought Rebecca. "She can sew better than any girl. She does many things better than I. I think Aunt Miranda wishes that Hannah had come."

But Hannah was needed at the farm. Aunt Miranda did not want Rebecca to come. She thought Rebecca was like her father, Lorenzo. She did not like him. He did not make a lot of money. She thought Rebecca's mother could have married a better man.

Rebecca did not like to sew the brown dress. All her dresses were brown!

She asked Aunt Miranda if she could please get some pink cloth.

"I think pink would be nice," said Rebecca.

Aunt Miranda got angry. She wished that Hannah could have come.

"I do not think that pink is nice," said Aunt Miranda. "Brown will have to do!"

"But pink cloth is no more money than brown," said Rebecca. "The man at the store said so!"

Now Aunt Miranda got real angry. She thought Rebecca was out of place. Rebecca was always making her angry. She did not put her things away. She went on errands and always forgot something. She

forgot to clean her room. She would put out the cat . . . and then she could not find him.

"How I wish that Hannah had come," thought Aunt Miranda.

Aunt Jane was sad for Rebecca. She had some words with her sister.

One day, Aunt Jane called Rebecca in from play.

"Go to your room, Rebecca," said Aunt Jane. "There is something there for you."

Rebecca ran to her room. There was her new, pink cloth!

"You are the sun in this dark, sad house," said Rebecca. "I will love you always."

AUNT JANE BRINGS SUNSHINE

COMPREHENSION CHECK

Choose the best answer.

1. In the beginning of this story, we learn that Rebecca
   ___a. showed Aunt Jane how to sew.
   ___b. can sew better than any girl.
   ___c. thinks her sister Hannah is better than she is.
   ___d. showed Hannah how to sew.

2. Hannah could not go to live with Aunts Miranda and Jane because
   ___a. she was too young.
   ___b. she did not know how to do anything.
   ___c. she was not wanted by the two aunts.
   ___d. she was needed on the farm to help her mother.

3. We find out in this story that Aunt Miranda
   ___a. did not want Rebecca to come and live with them.
   ___b. did not know how to sew.
   ___c. did not like Hannah.
   ___d. did not like the color brown.

4. Aunt Miranda did not like Rebecca because
   ___a. Rebecca was pretty.
   ___b. Rebecca was like her father.
   ___c. Rebecca was a mean, little girl.
   ___d. Rebecca was a cry baby.

5. Why didn't Aunt Miranda like Lorenzo?
   ___a. Because he did not make a lot of money.
   ___b. Because he did not marry her.
   ___c. Because he was very nice-looking.
   ___d. Because he had a lot of money.

6. When Rebecca asked if she could have some pink cloth, Aunt Miranda
   ___a. went out to buy her some right away.
   ___b. said she could have other colors too.
   ___c. got angry and said no.
   ___d. started to cry.

7. Aunt Jane was sad for Rebecca because
   ___a. Aunt Miranda was not very kind to Rebecca.
   ___b. Rebecca looked like her father.
   ___c. Rebecca liked the color pink.
   ___d. Rebecca broke her leg.

8. What is the "sunshine" that Aunt Jane brings to Rebecca?
   ___a. More brown cloth
   ___b. Hannah
   ___c. A cat
   ___d. Some pink cloth

9. Another name for this story could be
   ___a. "How To Sew."
   ___b. "A Trip To The Store."
   ___c. "A Pink Surprise."
   ___d. "A Clean Room."

10. This story is mainly about
    ___a. brown cloth.
    ___b. Aunt Miranda's feelings for Rebecca.
    ___c. Rebecca's sister Hannah.
    ___d. Rebecca's friends.

Check your answers with with key on page 67.

AUNT JANE BRINGS SUNSHINE

VOCABULARY CHECK

always	angry	nice	than	wish

I.   Sentences to Finish

Fill in the blank in each sentence with the correct key word from the box above.

1. I will _____ be your friend.

2. It is your birthday, what did you _____ for?

3. Mother was _____ with me because I came home late.

4. It was _____ of you to help me.

5. Bob is taller _____ my brother.

II.   Crossword Puzzle

Use the words from the box above to fill in the puzzle. Use the meanings below to help you choose the right answer.

Across

1. very fine
3. all the time
5. compared to

Down

2. to hope for something
4. to be mad

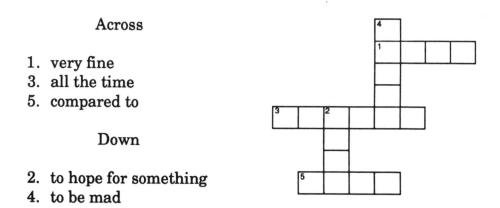

Check your answers with the key on page 69.

THE PINK DRESS

PREPARATION

Key Words

anything (en´ ē thing) any thing; thing of any kind
John will eat <u>anything</u> but liver.

let (let) to allow; permit
John will <u>let</u> the dog out.

listen (lis´n) try to hear
Mother would <u>listen</u> for her baby's cry.

shoe (shü) an outer covering for a person's foot
Jane put the left <u>shoe</u> on her right foot.

stay (stā) to remain in a place
Mary will <u>stay</u> home and wait for John.

THE PINK DRESS

Necessary Words

children	(chil′ drən)	young boys and girls *The <u>children</u> went out to play.*
Friday	(frī′ de)	the sixth day of the week *On <u>Friday</u>, we will have a party in school.*
mind	(mīnd)	feel bad about; object to *Would you <u>mind</u> if I did not go?*
sneak	(snēk)	to move in a secret way; to act like a person who does not want to be seen *Mom does not like when I <u>sneak</u> a cookie before dinner.*
soon	(sün)	in a short time; before long *<u>Soon</u> it will be dark.*

THE PINK DRESS

The class was going to read to some of Miss Dearborn's friends. All the children wanted to look special.

Preview:	1. Read the name of the story.
	2. Look at the picture.
	3. Read the sentences under the picture.
	4. Read the first two paragraphs of the story.
	5. Then answer the following question.

You learned from your preview that
___ a. Rebecca could not read.
___ b. Rebecca loved to read.
___ c. Rebecca did not like to read.
___ d. Rebecca was learning how to read.

Turn to the Comprehension Check on page 28 for the right answer.

Now read the story.

Read to find out about the day when Rebecca wears her new pink dress.

THE PINK DRESS

Rebecca loved to read. When she would read, the children would listen. They did not like to read. They did not read well. On Fridays, Miss Dearborn made the children read out loud.

Rebecca showed the children how to read. She made it fun. Soon, the children could read anything!

One day, Miss Dearborn let some friends come listen to the children read. Rebecca was glad. She wished she had sewn her pink dress. She wanted to look her best.

At lunch, Rebecca went home to eat. She went to her room. There was the pink dress! Aunt Jane had sewn it for her. Now she could look really nice. She didn't ask Aunt Miranda if she could put on the dress. No one was home. Rebecca didn't think she would mind.

The reading went well. The children liked to read . . . for Rebecca made it fun!

When Rebecca got home, Aunt Miranda was angry.

"You put on your new dress," said Aunt Miranda. "And you did not ask me."

"No one was home. I didn't think you would mind," said Rebecca. "I wanted to look nice this day. So I put on my new dress and shoes."

Aunt Miranda put Rebecca to bed. She could not have anything to eat.

Rebecca wanted to run away. She would go home and let Hannah stay here. Rebecca did not want to stay here.

When Aunt Miranda was not looking, Rebecca ran to Mr. Cobb's house.

He listened to Rebecca and how she wanted to go home.

"I think you had better stay," said Mr. Cobb. "Aunt Miranda could get VERY angry. Then she will not let Hannah come. And Aunt Miranda gives you good food to eat. She gives you nice clothes and shoes. She put you in a good school. And what will Miss Dearborn think? And Aunt Jane?" he said.

Rebecca thought she had better stay. Mr. Cobb helped Rebecca sneak home.

In her room, Rebecca was thinking.

"I will get Aunt Miranda to like me," she thought.

"I will find a way."

27

THE PINK DRESS

COMPREHENSION CHECK

Choose the best answer.

1. Rebecca showed the children in her class how to
   ___a. cook.
   ___b. sew.
   ___c. read.
   ___d. sing.

2. Because the children could read so well now, Miss Dearborn
   ___a. let them read to some of her friends.
   ___b. gave them the day off.
   ___c. gave them more homework.
   ___d. told them they did not have to come to school any more.

3. Rebecca wanted to wear her pink dress because
   ___a. it was her birthday.
   ___b. she wanted to look really nice for school.
   ___c. she was going to the circus.
   ___d. she was having her picture taken.

4. Why didn't Rebecca ask her aunt if she could wear the pink dress?
   ___a. Rebecca never asked to do anything.
   ___b. She knew they would say no.
   ___c. She bought the dress with her own money.
   ___d. No one was home.

5. When Rebecca got home from school wearing her pink dress, Aunt Miranda
   ___a. told her how nice she looked.
   ___b. sent her to bed with nothing to eat.
   ___c. took her picture.
   ___d. hit her.

6. Rebecca wanted to run away so she
   ___a. ran to Aunt Jane.
   ___b. ran all the way home.
   ___c. ran to Mr. Cobb's house.
   ___d. ran to Miss Dearborn.

7. After Mr. Cobb listened to Rebecca's story, he
   ___a. called Aunt Miranda.
   ___b. took Rebecca back to Sunnybrook Farm.
   ___c. told Rebecca she could live with him and Mrs. Cobb.
   ___d. told Rebecca she should go back to her aunts.

8. Mr. Cobb helped Rebecca sneak back to her aunt's house because
   ___a. he felt bad for her.
   ___b. Mrs. Cobb would yell at him.
   ___c. it was fun.
   ___d. Mrs. Cobb would yell at Rebecca.

9. Another name for this story could be
   ___a. "How To Read."
   ___b. "A Long Ride Home."
   ___c. "A Sad Day For Rebecca."
   ___d. "How To Sew."

10. This story is mainly about
    ___a. reading to the teacher.
    ___b. Rebecca and Aunt Miranda.
    ___c. Miss Dearborn's friends.
    ___d. Aunt Jane.

Check your answers with with key on page 67.

THE PINK DRESS

VOCABULARY CHECK

anything	let	listen	shoe	stay

I.   **Sentences to Finish**

Fill in the blank in each sentence with the correct key word from the box above.

1. Because we did not _____ to her, our teacher gave us a lot of homework.

2. "Please _____ me have another cookie," asked the little girl.

3. I will teach my brother how to tie his _____ .

4. Will you _____ with me for a little while?

5. Dad told me I could have _____ I want for my birthday.

II.   **Word Search**

All the words from the box above are hidden in the puzzle below. They may be written from left to right or up and down. As you find each word, put a circle around it. One word, that is not a key word, has been done for you.

```
W   A   Z   T   S   H   O   E
B   N   O   Z   L   C   F   J
X   Y   L   I   S   T   E   N
Q   T   A   W   H   I   K   L
Z   H   O   N   T   U   L   G
R   I   G   J   L   K   E   O
B   N   M   P   R   Q   T   N
L   G   S   T   A   Y   G   E
```

Check your answers with the key on page 70.

THE SIMPSONS GET A LAMP

PREPARATION

Key Words

both	(bōth)	the two; two together *Both boys will go to school.*
going	(gō´ ing)	leaving *Jane will be going to the store with Mother.*
lamp	(lamp)	an object that gives off light *We turn off the lamp when we go to sleep.*
outside	(out´ sīd´)	the side or surface that is out *When it is cold outside, I wear a hat.*
take	(tāk)	lay hold of; do; make *Mother makes me take a nap every day.*

THE SIMPSONS GET A LAMP

Necessary Words

People

Adam Ladd	A man about 30 years old that Rebecca met on her travels.
Clara Belle Simpson	One of the Simpson girls and Rebecca's friend.
Susan Simpson	Clara Belle's younger sister.

Places

jail	A prison. A place you go to stay in when you break the law. Mr. Simpson can often be found there.

Things

again	(ə gen´)	another time; once more *I have to do this <u>again</u> and <u>again</u> to do it right.*
company	(kum´ pə nē)	a number of persons united together for business; someone who comes to visit you *The hat <u>company</u> sells hats.*
idea	(ī dē´ ə)	a plan or a picture in the mind *I came up with an <u>idea</u> to make money.*
soap	(sōp)	something used to clean things or to wash with *I didn't wash my hands and face because the <u>soap</u> was gone.*
Thanksgiving Day	(thangks giv´ ing)	a holiday we celebrate in November *<u>Thanksgiving Day</u> is the day on which we give thanks for all we have.*

THE SIMPSONS GET A LAMP

Rebecca and Emma Jane set out to help get something nice for the Simpsons.

Preview: 1. Read the name of the story.
2. Look at the picture.
3. Read the sentence under the picture.
4. Read the first paragraph of the story.
5. Then answer the following question.

You learned from your preview that the Simpson children were
___ a. having a party.
___ b. moving.
___ c. sad.
___ d. very happy.

Turn to the Comprehension Check on page 34 for the right answer.

Now read the story.

Read to find out what Rebecca is up to.

THE SIMPSONS GET A LAMP

Thanksgiving Day would soon come. It was cold outside. The Simpson children were sad. They wanted a nice Thanksgiving. But there was not much money. Mr. Simpson was in jail. Mrs. Simpson would take in sewing so her children could eat. There was not enough food.

Susan and Clara Belle Simpson had an idea. They would make Thanksgiving a happy day. They would work for the soap company. If they could sell a lot of soap, they could get a lamp. It would be nice to have a new lamp.

Rebecca and Emma Jane heard of the idea. They wanted to help. They would both help the Simpsons get the lamp.

The girls went to the store. Outside, they put the soap in the coach. There were 300 bars of soap!

"It will take work to sell all this soap," said Emma Jane. "We had better get going, Rebecca."

In the morning, they both got going. They went house-to-house with the soap. Rebecca went to one house. Emma Jane went to the other. Rebecca sold more soap than Emma Jane. Rebecca had a way with words!

Rebecca saw a man sitting outside his house.

"What have you got there?" said the man.

"I'm selling soap. If I sell lots of soap, my friends can get a lamp," she said.

The man liked her. He thought it was nice of her to help her friends.

"How many soaps will you need Mr . . . "

"Adam Ladd is my name," said the man. "And what is yours?"

"My name is Rebecca Randall," answered Rebecca.

Rebecca liked Mr. Ladd. They talked for a long time. Mr. Ladd liked Rebecca very much.

"Tell you what," Adam said. "My aunt could use some soap. How much soap do you have?"

"We have 300 bars. How many would you like?"

"I'll take all 300 bars," said Adam.

Rebecca jumped!

"Oh, Mr. Ladd. You are so very nice. I must go tell Emma Jane. Now the Simpsons can get their lamp!"

Mr. Ladd was glad that he could help. He knew he would see Rebecca again.

THE SIMPSONS GET A LAMP

COMPREHENSION CHECK

Preview Answer:

c. sad.

Choose the best answer.

1. The Simpson children needed help because
   ___a. they didn't have money or food.
   ___b. they were moving.
   ___c. they were painting their house.
   ___d. they were having a party.

2. Susan and Clara Belle had an idea to
   ___a. run away from home.
   ___b. plant a garden.
   ___c. sell soap.
   ___d. chop down trees.

3. Rebecca and Emma Jane sold soap because they
   ___a. also needed food.
   ___b. wanted to help the Simpsons.
   ___c. wanted to make money.
   ___d. had nothing else to do.

4. If they could sell all the soap, they could get
   ___a. a new car.
   ___b. a wagon full of food.
   ___c. a color T.V.
   ___d. a new lamp.

5. Rebecca sold more soap than Emma Jane because
   ___a. she had a way with words.
   ___b. she knew more people.
   ___c. she had a bigger family.
   ___d. she tried harder.

6. Mr. Ladd liked Rebecca because
   ___a. she was pretty.
   ___b. she talked a lot.
   ___c. he liked to buy soap.
   ___d. he thought it was nice of her to try to help her friends.

7. To Rebecca's surpise, Mr. Ladd
   ___a. closed the door in her face.
   ___b. bought all 300 bars of soap.
   ___c. didn't have any food or money.
   ___d. told the girls to get off his land.

8. Mr. Ladd bought the soap because
   ___a. he felt bad for the girls and wanted to help them.
   ___b. he needed some soap.
   ___c. he was going to sell soap too!
   ___d. his aunt told him to buy all the soap.

9. Another name for this story could be
   ___a. "Too Much Soap."
   ___b. "A Wagon Ride."
   ___c. "Rebecca and Emma Get Going."
   ___d. "Soap For Sale."

10. This story is mainly about
    ___a. all kinds of soap.
    ___b. making new friends.
    ___c. helping friends.
    ___d. how to buy a lamp.

Check your answers with with key on page 67.

THE SIMPSONS GET A LAMP

VOCABULARY CHECK

both	going	lamp	outside	take

I. Sentences to Finish

Fill in the blank in each sentence with the correct key word from the box above.

1. I am not _____ to school today.

2. It was dark in the room so he turned on the _____ .

3. Will you _____ me with you?

4. Mom asked us _____ to stop talking.

5. At the zoo, most animals are _____ .

II. Mixed-up Words

Put the mixed-up letters of each word in the right order. Then draw a line from each word in Column A to its meaning in Column B.

Column A   Column B

1. gniog   _____   a. the side that is out

2. keat   _____   b. something that gives off light

3. usoited   _____   c. leaving

4. thob   _____   d. lay hold of

5. plam   _____   e. two together

Check your answers with the key on page 70.

A SAWYER AT LAST!

PREPARATION

Key Words

alike	(əlīk´)	similar; like one another *Jane and her mother look alike.*
around	(ə round´)	1. on all sides of; about *Tom chased his dog around the tree.* 2. near *Around October, the leaves begin to fall.*
brother	(bruŦHər)	a boy is brother to the other children of his parents *Tom and his brother shared the same room.*
felt	(felt)	1. had in one's mind *John felt sad that his dog was hurt.* 2. to feel; touch *Jane felt the cat's soft fur.*
milk	(milk)	1. the white liquid from cows *Mother buys fresh milk every day.* 2. to take the white liquid from a cow *Father gets up early to milk the cows.*

A SAWYER AT LAST!

Necessary Words

proud	(proud´)	thinking well of yourself
		Mom told me she is <u>proud</u> of everything I do.
visit	(viz´ it)	to stay with; to go to see
		Aunt Jane is coming to <u>visit</u> us.

Persons

Cousin Ann   The cousin that John goes to live with after her husband dies.

John   Rebecca's favorite and closest brother.

Reverend Burch   An old friend of the Sawyer family.

Mira   Rebecca's younger sister. Rebecca used to take care of Mira when she lived at Sunnybrook.

Places

church   A building where people meet to worship and pray to God.

A SAWYER AT LAST!

Rebecca gets the house ready for company.

Preview: 1. Read the name of the story.
2. Look at the picture.
3. Read the sentence under the picture.
4. Read the first paragraph of the story.
5. Then answer the following question.

You learned from your preview that
___ a. John went to live with Cousin Ann.
___ b. Cousin Ann went to live with Rebecca's mom.
___ c. Rebecca went to live with Cousin Ann.
___ d. Cousin Ann came to live with Rebecca.

Turn to the Comprehension Check on page 40 for the right answer.

Now read the story.

Read to find out how Rebecca shows that she is growing up.

A SAWYER AT LAST!

Two years had gone by. Rebecca had heard that her brother John wasn't living at home. Cousin Ann had lost her husband. John went to live with her. He helped her around the house. He would milk the cows and clean the barn. For his work, Cousin Ann put John in school. Rebecca felt glad for her brother.

When Rebecca's sister Mira died, Rebecca went home. She felt sad about Mira. She felt sad, too, that John wasn't around. She and John were very much alike. She missed him.

Hannah was growing up. "Soon she will be a woman," thought Rebecca. She felt bad for Hannah. "Hannah should be in school. Aunt Miranda wanted Hannah, but she got me. I can go to school and be something someday. But all Hannah has is the work on this farm."

Rebecca asked Hannah to take her place at Aunt Miranda's. But Hannah said no.

"Mother needs me here," said Hannah. "And I would not like school, Rebecca. You see, we are not alike. I am happy on the farm."

Rebecca went back to Riverboro. One morning, when her aunts were home with a cold, Rebecca went to church in their place.

"Be a good girl, Rebecca," said Aunt Miranda. "And let the church know we are sorry we could not come."

In church, Rebecca was asked to start the singing. She was afraid. But she was there in her aunts' place. She could not let them see that she was afraid.

When the singing was over, Rebecca felt proud. She never thought she could do that!

Reverend Burch and Mrs. Burch were in church. They had come for a visit. But they had no place to stay. Aunt Miranda was not happy when Rebecca told her they would be staying with them!

"How could you ask them to come here? You know we must stay in bed," said Aunt Miranda.

"Oh, just leave it to me, Aunt Miranda! I will do all the work. And it's only for two days!"

For two days, Rebecca did everything. She milked the cows. She cooked all the food! Aunt Miranda was so proud of her!

"She may be a Randall," thought Aunt Miranda. "But she's a Sawyer too!"

A SAWYER AT LAST!

COMPREHENSION CHECK

Choose the best answer.

1. Rebecca's brother John went to live with Cousin Ann because
   ___a. he ran away from home.
   ___b. she had lost her husband.
   ___c. no one loved him.
   ___d. Aunt Miranda sent him away.

2. In return for his hard work around the house, Cousin Ann sent John
   ___a. a new car.
   ___b. to school.
   ___c. a new toy.
   ___d. some money.

3. Rebecca felt bad for Hannah because she thought Hannah wanted to go to
   ___a. the dance.
   ___b. the store.
   ___c. Cousin Ann's.
   ___d. school.

4. Rebecca was surprised to find out that Hannah was
   ___a. going to the party.
   ___b. going to school.
   ___c. happy on the farm.
   ___d. going to live with Aunts Miranda and Jane.

5. Back in Riverboro, Rebecca went to church in place of her two aunts. In church, Rebecca was asked to sing. At first, she felt
   ___a. afraid.
   ___b. happy.
   ___c. silly.
   ___d. proud.

6. When church was over, Rebecca felt
   ___a. very sad.
   ___b. proud of herself.
   ___c. very silly.
   ___d. like crying.

7. At first, when Rebecca told Aunt Miranda that the Reverend and Mrs. Burch were going to spend two nights with them,
   ___a. Aunt Miranda was not happy.
   ___b. Aunt Miranda was very happy.
   ___c. Aunt Miranda sent Rebecca to her room.
   ___d. Aunt Miranda began to plan a big party.

8. Aunt Miranda was proud of Rebecca because
   ___a. Rebecca went away to school.
   ___b. Rebecca could dance well.
   ___c. Rebecca could cook well.
   ___d. Rebecca had worked very hard without being told to.

9. Another name for this story could be
   ___a. "A Day in Church."
   ___b. "Rebecca Wins Aunt Miranda's Love."
   ___c. "Life With Cousin Ann."
   ___d. "Lucky John."

10. This story is mainly about
    ___a. Rebecca going to church.
    ___b. Rebecca and Hannah.
    ___c. Rebecca showing that she is growing up.
    ___d. Rebecca feeling bad.

Check your answers with with key on page 67.

A SAWYER AT LAST!

VOCABULARY CHECK

alike	around	brother	felt	milk

I.   Sentences to Finish

Fill in the blank in each sentence with the correct key word from the box above.

1. There are three children in my family; my sister, my _____ , and me.

2. All babies need _____ to grow.

3. When I saw the balloons, I _____ happy.

4. Has my dog been _____ here today?

5. Those twins sure do look _____ .

II.   Crossword Puzzle

Use the words from the box above to fill in the puzzle. The meanings below will help you choose the right words.

Across

2. same; like one another
4. not my sister, but my _____

Down

1.   to feel
2.   to be near
3.   cows give us this

Check your answers with the key on page 70.

REBECCA GOES TO WAREHAM

PREPARATION

Key Words

game   (gām)   1. a way of playing
                                John and Mary will play a <u>game</u> of tag.
                        2. to make fun of or laugh at
                                *John did not do well in school. He thought
                                school was just a <u>game</u>.*

herself   (hér selfˇ)   herself is used instead of she or her:
                                        1. Mary hurt <u>herself</u>.
                                        2. Mary can do it <u>herself</u>.

lazy   (lā´ zē)   not willing to work; not very active
                                *Mary thought John was <u>lazy</u> because he
                                never cleaned his room.*

maybe   (mā´ bē)   possibly; perhaps
                                *John works real hard. <u>Maybe</u> one day he will
                                be president.*

never   (nev´ ər)   not ever; at no time
                                Jane would <u>never</u> tell a lie.

REBECCA GOES TO WAREHAM

Necessary Words

cane	(kān)	a stick that is used to help people walk *My grandfather uses a cane to help him walk.*
married	(mar´ ēd)	to be joined as husband and wife *Ann and my brother were married last week.*
newspaper	(nüz´ pā´ pər)	sheets of printed paper that tell stories or news *I try to read the newspaper every day.*
private	(prī´ vit)	just for a few special people; not for the public *We are going to have a private meeting.*
save	(sāv)	to make safe; to keep from harm, danger, or loss; to put aside for later use. *I tried to save the puppy from being hit by the car.*
writer/writing	(rī´ tər)	1. a person who writes 2. the act of making words with a pen, pencil, etc. *When I grow up, I want to be a writer.*

People

Miss Emily Maxwell One of Rebecca's teachers and a good friend.

Places

Wareham A large town not far from Riverboro. The town where Rebecca goes to school.

REBECCA GOES TO WAREHAM

Rebecca loved to read. She wanted to learn all that she could.

Preview: 1. Read the name of the story.
2. Look at the picture.
3. Read the sentences under the picture.
4. Read the first paragraph of the story.
5. Then answer the following question.

You learned from your preview that
___ a. Rebecca did not want to go to Wareham.
___ b. Rebecca did not like school.
___ c. Rebecca was not lazy in her school work.
___ d. Rebecca had lots of money.

Turn to the Comprehension Check on page 46 for the right answer.

Now read the story.

Read to find out about Rebecca and her new school.

REBECCA GOES TO WAREHAM

Rebecca never thought she would get to Wareham. She was very proud of herself. The Wareham school was not like her other schools. It was a private school. It took a lot of money to send Rebecca there. But she did well in school. She was not lazy in her work. Aunt Miranda and Aunt Jane would find a way to get the money. Rebecca was 15 years old now. In three years, her schooling would be over.

Rebecca never thought school a game. She was not a lazy girl. She worked night and day to be the best she could be. When other girls were looking at boys, Rebecca would read. She thought it better to read than play games with the boys.

One of her teachers, Miss Emily Maxwell, liked Rebecca. She never saw a child work so hard. She could read so well! And she could write! Maybe she could be a writer!

"Maybe she could work for the school paper," she thought.

It did not take long! Rebecca soon became the school's best writer. She liked writing for the school paper. The Wareham school was getting to know Rebecca Randall!

Rebecca felt happy for herself. But she felt bad for Aunt Miranda. She had been sick. It was hard for her to get around. She had to walk with a cane now.

Back home at Sunnybrook Farm, things were not well. It had been a bad year on the farm. There was not enough to eat. There was very little money. Rebecca's mother was now sick, and Hannah would be leaving soon to get married.

"Who will help my sister with the farm?" thought Aunt Miranda. "Hannah will be going away. How will my sister get money for the farm?"

Hannah came to Riverboro for a visit. Aunt Miranda was not happy with Hannah. Hannah only thought of herself. She wanted to get married. She should help her mother with the farm. Aunt Miranda was glad to see Hannah leave.

Aunt Miranda was sure that if the farm was to be saved, Rebecca was the one to save it!

REBECCA GOES TO WAREHAM

COMPREHENSION CHECK

Choose the best answer.

1. The Wareham school
   ___a. was very far from Riverboro.
   ___b. was not a very good school.
   ___c. was a private school.
   ___d. was open to everyone.

2. Rebecca worked hard
   ___a. to be the best she could be.
   ___b. on her singing.
   ___c. on the farm.
   ___d. at the candy store.

3. Miss Emily Maxwell thought
   ___a. Rebecca was not a good person.
   ___b. Rebecca could be a writer.
   ___c. Rebecca was in danger.
   ___d. Rebecca was lazy.

4. Rebecca made a name for herself by
   ___a. running away from school.
   ___b. teaching at the school.
   ___c. fighting with everyone at school.
   ___d. writing for the school paper.

5. Even though Rebecca was happy for herself, she
   ___a. felt bad for Miss Maxwell.
   ___b. felt bad for Aunt Miranda.
   ___c. was not happy in school.
   ___d. was not feeling well.

6. Aunt Miranda
   ___a. was still mean.
   ___b. was happy with Hannah.
   ___c. needed a cane to walk now.
   ___d. went to stay at Sunnybrook.

7. Back home at Sunnybrook Farm,
   ___a. things were not well.
   ___b. Rebecca's mother was fine.
   ___c. there was plenty of food and money.
   ___d. everything was fine.

8. Aunt Miranda was afraid that Rebecca's mother
   ___a. would never take Rebecca back.
   ___b. would never come to see Rebecca.
   ___c. would not let Hannah get married.
   ___d. would lose Sunnybrook Farm.

9. Another name for this story could be
   ___a. "A Happy Day for Hannah."
   ___b. "Hard-Working Rebecca."
   ___c. "The Best Teacher."
   ___d. "Lazy Rebecca."

10. This story is mainly about
    ___a. Rebecca's sister Hannah.
    ___b. Rebecca's mother.
    ___c. Rebecca playing games in school.
    ___d. Rebecca trying to be the best she can be.

Check your answers with with key on page 67.

REBECCA GOES TO WAREHAM

VOCABULARY CHECK

game	herself	lazy	maybe	never

I. Sentences to Finish

Fill in the blank in each sentence with the correct key word from the box above.

1. She tried to move the big box all by _____ .

2. Mother said that _____ I can go to the party on Saturday.

3. All the children wanted to play a _____ .

4. My brother _____ lets me play with his baseball bat.

5. Dad said I was _____ because I never put my things away.

II. Mixed-up Words

Put the mixed-up letters of each word in the right order. Then draw a line from each word in Column A to its meaning in Column B.

Column A

1. reven _____

2. shelfer _____

3. zaly _____

4. meag _____

5. beamy _____

Column B

a. not willing to work

b. perhaps

c. at no time

d. a way of playing

e. used in place of she or her

Check your answers with the key on page 71.

THE BIG DAY!

PREPARATION

Key Words

an	(an)	one; any *Is there an apple for me?*
garden	(gärd´ n)	ground used for growing flowers, vegetables or fruit. *Mother plants seeds in the garden every spring.*
hurry	(her´ ē)	to move quickly *We must hurry to school before we are late.*
sky	(skī)	the covering over the world; the area of the clouds or the upper air *There are many stars in the sky at night.*
you're	(yür)	you are *If you're cold, put on your coat.*

THE BIG DAY!

Necessary Words

move   (müv)   to put or keep in motion; shake; stir
> *I cannot <u>move</u> my arm; it hurts too much.*

parade   (pə rād´)   a group of people walking for display or show
> *I like to watch a <u>parade</u>.*

prize   (prīz)
1. a reward
2. something you win after trying against other people
> *The <u>prize</u> for winning the race was a baseball bat.*

stroke   (strōk)   a sudden attack (of disease)
> *A <u>stroke</u> can cause the body to lose its ability to move.*

watch   (woch)   to look at something carefully
> *It is fun to <u>watch</u> butterflies fly.*

THE BIG DAY!

Rebecca's last day at Wareham was going to be a beautiful one.

Preview:
1. Read the name of the story.
2. Look at the picture.
3. Read the sentence under the picture.
4. Read the first paragraph of the story.
5. Then answer the following question.

You learned from your preview that Adam Ladd
___ a. made sure all the writing prizes were money.
___ b. made sure all the money went to the farm.
___ c. did not have any friends.
___ d. did not think Rebecca was a very good writer.

Turn to the Comprehension Check on page 52 for the right answer.

Now read the story.

Read to find out about Rebecca's last day at the Wareham school.

THE BIG DAY!

Rebecca's writing had won her many prizes in school. She didn't know that it was Adam Ladd who made sure each prize would be money. He had many friends at Wareham. He was sure Rebecca's writing could take the prizes. He knew how much she needed the money for the farm.

Rebecca was 17 years old now. It was time for her to leave school. All her friends were there for the big day. Adam Ladd, the Cobbs, Hannah and her husband, Cousin Ann, and John sat in the garden. It was a fine day. The sky was blue.

They all watched Rebecca in the parade. She had on an old dress. But she looked finer than any of the other girls.

"You're going to make a fine woman," thought Adam.

When the parade was over, she saw Adam in the garden.

"How did I do?" she asked him.

"You're really some girl," said Adam. "You were the best-looking girl in the parade!"

Rebecca looked around. She was sure Aunt Miranda was not coming. But where was Aunt Jane? She was sure Aunt Jane was coming.

Then, she saw the Cobbs coming. They looked like they were in a hurry.

"We are sorry, Rebecca," said Jeremiah. "Aunt Jane could not come. Aunt Miranda has had a stroke. She can't move her arms or legs. But she can still talk. Aunt Jane is with her now."

Rebecca wanted to hurry home. She wanted to tell Aunt Miranda that she would stay with her. She would not leave her to teach at the school far away. She would stay and teach here!

Aunt Miranda would not listen to Rebecca.

"You listen to me," she said. "You're to go teach at the best school. Don't let an old woman like me keep you here in this place. Now you go on out and do what is best for YOU!"

Rebecca ran from the house. She wanted to be by herself. She looked up at the sky. Rebecca felt very sad.

"Why is it so sad to grow old?" she thought.

THE BIG DAY!

COMPREHENSION CHECK

Choose the best answer.

1. In school, Rebecca won many prizes for
    ___a. riding horses.
    ___b. baking.
    ___c. singing.
    ___d. writing stories.

2. Adam Ladd made sure the prizes were always money because
    ___a. he knew how much Rebecca needed money for the farm.
    ___b. he wanted Rebecca to have nice clothes.
    ___c. he wanted Rebecca to buy a car.
    ___d. he could not think of anything else to give.

3. Adam Ladd told Rebecca
    ___a. he loved her.
    ___b. she was the best-looking girl in the parade.
    ___c. he could never see her again.
    ___d. that he was the one who made sure all the prizes were money.

4. Many of Rebecca's friends and family came to see her in the parade. Who didn't?
    ___a. The Cobbs
    ___b. Hannah
    ___c. Her aunts Miranda and Jane
    ___d. Cousin Ann

5. Aunt Jane did not see Rebecca on her last day of school because
    ___a. Aunt Miranda had a stroke.
    ___b. Aunt Miranda would not let her go.
    ___c. she did not care about Rebecca.
    ___d. she thought parades were silly.

6. Rebecca told Aunt Miranda that
    ___a. she did not want to stay in Riverboro.
    ___b. she did not love her aunts.
    ___c. she would stay with her and take care of her.
    ___d. she would marry Adam Ladd.

7. Aunt Miranda told Rebecca to
    ___a. never leave her.
    ___b. go out and teach at the best school.
    ___c. go back to Sunnybrook Farm.
    ___d. go out and spend all the prize money on herself.

8. Aunt Miranda did not want Rebecca to stay and take care of her because
    ___a. she wanted her to do something special with her life.
    ___b. she did not like Rebecca.
    ___c. Hannah was going to take care of her.
    ___d. she was all better now.

9. Another name for this story could be
    ___a. "A New Life for Rebecca."
    ___b. "More Prizes!"
    ___c. "The Big Parade."
    ___d. "School Days."

10. This story is mainly about
    ___a. having a parade.
    ___b. private schools.
    ___c. Rebecca's last day at school.
    ___d. Adam Ladd.

Check your answers with with key on page 67.

THE BIG DAY!

VOCABULARY CHECK

an	garden	hurry	sky	you're

I.   Sentences to Finish

Fill in the blank in each sentence with the correct key word from the box above.

1. This year, I am going to plant corn in my _____ .

2. I must _____ or I will miss the bus.

3. We hope that _____ going to come to see us in the play.

4. The plane was flying high up in the _____ .

5. Would you like to have a balloon or _____ ice ceam?

II.   Word Use

Put a check next to YES if the sentence makes sense. Put a check next to NO if the sentence does not make sense.

1. I swim in the <u>garden</u> every day.   ___ YES ___ NO

2. If you are in a <u>hurry</u>, go slow.   ___ YES ___ NO

3. I am waiting for <u>an</u> answer.   ___ YES ___ NO

4. <u>You're</u> coat is on the floor.   ___ YES ___ NO

5. The <u>sky</u> is a beautiful blue today.   ___ YES ___ NO

Check your answers with the key on page 71.

MORE RAIN FOR REBECCA

PREPARATION

Key Words

any   (en´ ē)   some or one; even a little
        Would you care for <u>any</u> fresh fruit?

most   (mōst)   1. greatest in amount
        Mother was <u>most</u> proud of her garden.
        2. almost all
        Mary ate <u>most</u> of her ice cream.

six   (siks)   one more than five; 6
        We eat supper at <u>six</u> o'clock.

soft   (sôft)   not hard; smooth; not loud
        A new baby has very <u>soft</u> skin.

why   (hwī)   for what reason?
        <u>Why</u> did the baby cry?

MORE RAIN FOR REBECCA

Necessary Words

change   (chānj)   put something in place of another
We waited for Dad to change his shirt.

just   (just)   1. a very little while ago
He just left me.
2. exactly
Just then, it started to rain.

letter   (let´ ər)   a group of words that carry a message
I just mailed a letter to my friend.

life   (līf)   living; being alive
Grandmother told me that her life had been filled with joy.

railroad   (rāl´ rōd´)   the tracks, stations, trains, and people who manage them
Years ago, my grandfather worked for the railroad.

thank   (thangk)   to feel grateful; to show that you are grateful
Say "thank you" when someone does something nice for you.

MORE RAIN FOR REBECCA

Rebecca gets news from Sunnybrook that will change her plans.

Preview: 1. Read the name of the story.
2. Look at the picture.
3. Read the sentence under the picture.
4. Read the first paragraph of the story.
5. Then answer the following question.

You learned from your preview that
___ a. Rebecca never wanted to leave Riverboro.
___ b. Rebecca wanted to get on with her life.
___ c. Aunt Miranda was going to Sunnybrook.
___ d. Aunts Jane and Miranda had a fight.

Turn to the Comprehension Check on page 58 for the right answer.

Now read the story.

Read to find out what happens when Rebecca is all ready to go out on her own.

MORE RAIN FOR REBECCA

Aunt Miranda was getting better every day. Rebecca felt that she could soon leave Riverboro. She had lived with the Sawyers for more than six years. She wanted so much to get on with her life.

The time had come. Rebecca kissed her aunts and thanked them for all their help. For over six years, this had been her home. She would miss them. She would miss Aunt Jane the most.

Just then, a boy walked up to the house. He had a letter for Rebecca. It was from Hannah. It read:

Dear Rebecca,

Mother fell down in the barn. She can't walk. Come home - and hurry.

Hannah

Rebecca went home to the farm. Aunt Miranda was most angry. "Why is Rebecca always needed to help out?" she thought. "Can't any of the other children help out? Why can't Rebecca get to do anything for herself? She has wanted to teach for a long time . . . and now this!"

Aunt Miranda had a long talk with Jane.

". . . and when I am gone," said Aunt Miranda, "I want Rebecca to have this house. But don't you tell her now Jane. I don't want to be thanked! I am sure she will change lots of things around here. Maybe put some color into the place. Some soft pinks . . . if I know Rebecca! Well . . . maybe when I am gone, I will not mind!"

Rebecca worked hard to help her mother. She cooked, sewed, and cleaned the house. She milked the cows and cleaned the barn. When she was not working, she would read to her mother.

One day, Mrs. Randall looked down at Rebecca's hands. They were not soft as most girls' hands were. Mrs. Randall was sad.

"I am sorry Rebecca," said her mother. "I am keeping you from a good life."

"No, Mother," said Rebecca. "I am just a little girl. I have lots of years to live my life. So do not be sad for me."

Soon, a letter came from Aunt Jane. Aunt Miranda had died. "Please come," it said, "if your mother is well enough."

As Rebecca waited for the train, she saw Adam Ladd. He thought Rebecca looked very sad. He wanted to tell her that the railroad was going to buy the farm for a lot of money! That she would never have any worries about the farm again. But when he looked at her, he knew that she was not sad about the farm. Her sad face did not have a thing to do with money.

MORE RAIN FOR REBECCA

COMPREHENSION CHECK

Choose the best answer.

<table>
<tr><td>Preview Answer:</td></tr>
<tr><td>b. Rebecca wanted to get on with her life.</td></tr>
</table>

1. In this story, we find out that Rebecca
   ___a. never liked living with her aunts.
   ___b. felt she could soon leave Riverboro.
   ___c. did not do well in school.
   ___d. loved the rain.

2. When the time came for Rebecca to leave her aunts' home, she
   ___a. thanked them for all their help.
   ___b. left without saying good-bye.
   ___c. told them she would not miss them.
   ___d. told them she never wanted to see them again.

3. Before Rebecca left,
   ___a. the house burned down.
   ___b. Adam Ladd married Aunt Jane.
   ___c. she paid her aunts back for her schooling.
   ___d. a letter came for her from Sunnybrook.

4. Rebecca had to go back to Sunnybrook because
   ___a. she had nowhere else to go.
   ___b. she got a job on the farm.
   ___c. her mother had fallen and could not walk.
   ___d. Adam Ladd told her to go home.

5. When Rebecca went back to Sunnybrook, Aunt Miranda was angry because
   ___a. she felt the other children should be able to help out.
   ___b. she wanted Rebecca to stay with her.
   ___c. Rebecca took her good pin.
   ___d. Rebecca took all the prize money with her.

6. Aunt Miranda told Aunt Jane that
   ___a. they had no more money.
   ___b. Adam Ladd wanted to marry her.
   ___c. she wanted to give the house to Rebecca.
   ___d. Rebecca was never going to be anything.

7. Aunt Miranda did not want Rebecca to know about the house until she died, because
   ___a. she could change her mind.
   ___b. she did not want Rebecca to thank her.
   ___c. Rebecca would laugh at her.
   ___d. she knew how much Rebecca did not like the house.

8. Rebecca's aunt left her the house because
   ___a. Aunt Jane did not want it.
   ___b. it needed to be fixed up.
   ___c. Adam Ladd told her to.
   ___d. she loved Rebecca.

9. Another name for this story could be
   ___a. "Aunt Miranda's Secret."
   ___b. "Happy Birthday, Mom."
   ___c. "Adam and Rebecca."
   ___d. "A Day On The Farm."

10. This story is mainly about
   ___a. a lot of rain in Riverboro.
   ___b. Rebecca's mother falling down.
   ___c. Adam and Rebecca meeting at the railroad.
   ___d. Aunt Miranda showing that she does love Rebecca.

Check your answers with the key on page 67.

MORE RAIN FOR REBECCA

VOCABULARY CHECK

any	most	six	soft	why

I. Sentences to Finish

Fill in the blank in each sentence with the correct key word from the box above.

1. John did _____ of the painting of the fence.

2. My sister is _____ years old today.

3. The teacher wants to know _____ I always forget my work.

4. Are there _____ cookies left?

5. A stone is hard; it is not _____ .

II. Word Search

All the words from the box above are hidden in the puzzle below. They may be written from left to right or up and down. As you find each word, put a circle around it. One word, that is not a key word, has been done for you.

M	I	P	R	Q	L	W	S
A	B	A	N	Y	C	T	O
W	C	D	F	L	R	S	F
M	G	M	Q	H	I	J	T
I	K	E	W	M	O	S	T
S	I	O	F	K	M	C	S
I	J	P	W	H	Y	D	A
X	H	N	B	A	F	G	T

Check your answers with the key on page 71.

A NEW HOME FOR REBECCA

PREPARATION

Key Words

act	(akt)	to behave like *Most people <u>act</u> silly now and then.*
ago	(əgō´)	1. gone by; passed *I met her two years <u>ago</u>.* 2. in the past *Grandfather was a fireman long <u>ago</u>.*
does	(duz)	to do; carries out *Mary <u>does</u> all her work well.*
grand	(grand)	large and fine; great *John lives in a <u>grand</u>, old house.*
sorry	(sor´ ē)	to feel bad about someone or something *John was <u>sorry</u> that he stepped on Mother's flowers.*

A NEW HOME FOR REBECCA

Necessary Words

dream/dreamed   (drēm)   something thought of or seen while sleeping; a thought
> *My dream is to be a great painter.*

mine   (mīn)   of me; belonging to me
> *That book is not yours; it is mine.*

right   (rīt)   at once; exactly
> *Come home, right now.*

wait   (wāt)   to stay until someone comes or something happens
> *I will wait for you to call me.*

while   (hwīl)   time; during the time that
> *I waited for you for a long while, but you never came.*

A NEW HOME FOR REBECCA

Aunt Jane tells Rebecca that Aunt Miranda was sorry for all the mean words she ever said to her.

Preview:	1. Read the name of the story.
	2. Look at the picture.
	3. Read the sentence under the picture.
	4. Read the first two paragraphs of the story.
	5. Then answer the following question.

You learned from your preview that

___ a. Rebecca was going away for good.

___ b. Rebecca was happy to go back to Riverboro.

___ c. Rebecca did not like Mr. Cobb.

___ d. Rebecca did not want to ever go back to Riverboro.

Turn to the Comprehension Check on page 64 for the right answer.

Now read the story.

Read to find out where Rebecca will make her home.

A NEW HOME FOR REBECCA

Rebecca waited for the stagecoach. It would take her back to Riverboro.

She was so happy when she saw that the driver was Mr. Cobb. He asked her if she would like to sit with him for the ride. She kissed him. She had missed him and the others so. The ride made her think of happy days of long ago.

Soon, they came to the Sawyer house. It was a grand, old house. Aunt Jane was waiting outside.

"She does look so old," thought Rebecca. "She must be sad to live in this big house by herself." Rebecca felt sorry for Aunt Jane.

"Don't go in to see Aunt Miranda right now," said Aunt Jane. "First, I want to tell you something. Your Aunt Miranda did not want to act mean. She could not help it. She just wanted what was best for you. I am sure she was sorry for every bad word she said to you. Look around Rebecca. Aunt Miranda left this grand, old house to you. This house, and all the things in it, are now yours."

Rebecca didn't know how to act. She did not know what to say.

"May I go in and see her now?" asked Rebecca.

Rebecca went into the house. She stayed there for a little while. When she came out, she felt a change in herself.

"Does this mean that this house is really mine?" she asked Aunt Jane.

"Yes, Rebecca, it does," said Aunt Jane.

"This is the house I dreamed of long ago. Now I will have my garden . . . and a place for Mother to stay. Mother will be with her sister again. She will have all the friends she has not seen for so long."

"Thank you Aunt Miranda," she said to herself. "Thank you for all that you did for me. I will always love you. I will always love this house, and I know I will love the house it will be."

A NEW HOME FOR REBECCA

COMPREHENSION CHECK

Choose the best answer.

<table>
<tr><td>Preview Answer:</td></tr>
<tr><td>b. Rebecca was happy to go back to Riverboro.</td></tr>
</table>

1. In the beginning of this story, we find that
   ___a. Rebecca missed Mr. Cobb and the others a lot.
   ___b. Rebecca was going back to school in Wareham.
   ___c. Mr. Cobb never did like Rebecca.
   ___d. Rebecca never did like Mr. Cobb.

2. To Rebecca, Aunt Jane looked
   ___a. happy.
   ___b. beautiful.
   ___c. old and sad.
   ___d. grand.

3. Rebecca thought that Aunt Jane
   ___a. was happy Aunt Miranda died.
   ___b. was not happy to see her come back to Riverboro.
   ___c. was going to have a party.
   ___d. was sad living in the big house by herself.

4. Aunt Jane told Rebecca that
   ___a. Aunt Miranda did not like her.
   ___b. Aunt Miranda had only wanted the best for Rebecca.
   ___c. Adam Ladd was looking for her.
   ___d. she must move out of the house right away.

5. To Rebecca's surprise,
   ___a. Aunt Miranda gave her the house and everything in it.
   ___b. Aunt Miranda came back to life.
   ___c. Aunt Jane left for good.
   ___d. Aunt Jane was angry with her.

6. Rebecca is happy that the big house is hers. She tells Aunt Jane
   ___a. to pack her things.
   ___b. she wants the house all to herself.
   ___c. that she plans to bring her mother here to live with them.
   ___d. that the house needs to be painted.

7. At the end of this story, we find out that
   ___a. Rebecca did not care about her mother.
   ___b. Rebecca always loved Aunt Miranda and the big house.
   ___c. Rebecca is going to sell the house and go back to Sunnybrook.
   ___d. Rebecca only cared about herself.

8. A lot of things happen to Rebecca in this story. We find Rebecca to be a girl who
   ___a. thinks of no one but herself.
   ___b. always thinks about her family first.
   ___c. does not think she needs to thank her aunts for anything.
   ___d. is not very kind.

9. Another name for this story could be
   ___a. "Forever Yours."
   ___b. "Back on the Farm Again."
   ___c. "Happy Days of Long Ago."
   ___d. "Rebecca Returns to Riverboro."

10. This story is mainly about
   ___a. Mr. Cobb and Rebecca.
   ___b. Rebecca running away.
   ___c. the change that takes place in Rebecca's life.
   ___d. Rebecca's mother getting better.

Check your answers with with key on page 67.

A NEW HOME FOR REBECCA

VOCABULARY CHECK

act	ago	does	grand	sorry

I. Sentences to Finish

Fill in the blank in each sentence with the correct key word from the box above.

1. "What a _____ time I had at the party," said Mary.

2. "Who _____ the dishes tonight?" asked Dad.

3. Your mother was looking for you a little while _____ .

4. Sometimes I like to _____ like a clown.

5. My brother said he was _____ for dropping Mom's lamp.

II. Matching

Write the letter of the correct meaning from Column B next to the key word in column A.

Column A

___ 1. grand

___ 2. act

___ 3. sorry

___ 4. ago

___ 5. does

Column B

a. to feel bad about something

b. in the past

c. to do

d. large and fine; great

e. to behave like

Check your answers with the key on page 72.

NOTES

COMPREHENSION CHECK ANSWER KEY
Lessons CTR-A-11 to CTR-A-20

LESSON NUMBER	QUESTION NUMBER										PAGE NUMBER
	1	2	3	4	5	6	7	8	9	10	
CTR-A-11	d	b	a	c	d	a	b	ⓒ	△a	☐d	10
CTR-A-12	a	b	d	b	a	c	ⓑ	c	△a	☐d	16
CTR-A-13	ⓒ	d	a	b	a	c	ⓐ	d	△c	☐b	22
CTR-A-14	c	a	b	d	b	c	d	ⓐ	△c	☐b	28
CTR-A-15	a	c	b	d	a	d	b	ⓐ	△d	☐c	34
CTR-A-16	b	b	d	c	a	b	a	ⓓ	△b	☐c	40
CTR-A-17	c	a	b	d	b	c	a	ⓓ	△b	☐d	46
CTR-A-18	d	a	b	c	a	c	b	ⓐ	△a	☐c	52
CTR-A-19	b	a	d	c	a	c	b	ⓓ	△a	☐d	58
CTR-A-20	a	c	d	b	a	c	b	ⓑ	△d	☐c	64

◯ = Inference (not said straight out, but you know from what is said)

△ = Another name for the story

☐ = Main idea of the story

NOTES

VOCABULARY CHECK ANSWER KEY

Lessons CTR A-11 to CTR A-20

LESSON NUMBER		PAGE NUMBER
11	REBECCA LEAVES THE FARM	11

I.
1. name
2. clean
3. fine
4. farm
5. horse

II.
1. c
2. e
3. a
4. b
5. d

12	REBECCA GOES TO SCHOOL	17

I.
1. miss
2. leave
3. barn
4. flowers
5. thought

II.
1. NO
2. NO
3. NO
4. YES
5. YES

13	AUNT JANE BRINGS SUNSHINE	23

I.
1. always
2. wish
3. angry
4. nice
5. than

II.

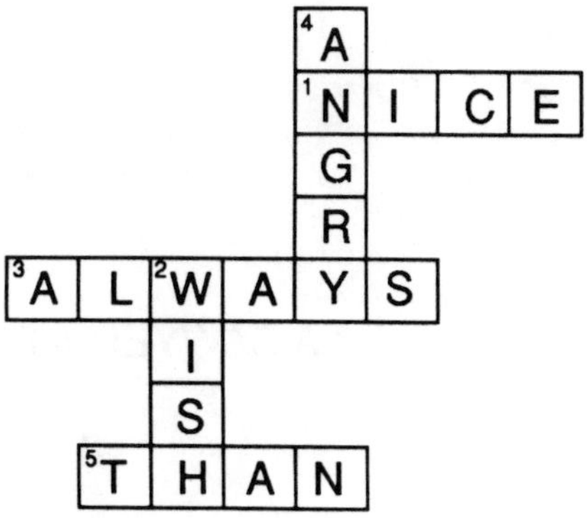

VOCABULARY CHECK ANSWER KEY

Lessons CTR A-11 to CTR A-20

14   THE PINK DRESS   29

I.   1. listen
    2. let
    3. shoe
    4. stay
    5. anything

II. 1.

```
W   A   Z   T   (S   H   O   E)
B   N   O   Z   L   C   F   J
X   Y  (L   I   S   T   E   N)
Q   T   A   W   H   I   K   L
Z   H   O   N   T   U  (L   G
R   I   G   J   L   K   E   O
B   N   M   P   R   Q   T)  N
L   G) (S   T   A   Y)  G   E
```

15   THE SIMPSONS GET A LAMP   35

I.   1. going
    2. lamp
    3. take
    4. both
    5. outside

II. 1. going, c
    2. take, d
    3. outside, a
    4. both, e
    5. lamp, b

16   A SAWYER AT LAST!   41

I.   1. brother
    2. milk
    3. felt
    4. around
    5. alike

II.

```
                          3M
             1F            I
              E            L
              L        2A  L  I  K  E
        4B  R  O  T  H  E  R
                          O
                          U
                          N
                          D
```

VOCABULARY CHECK ANSWER KEY

Lessons CTR A-11 to CTR A-20

LESSON NUMBER		PAGE NUMBER

17 REBECCA GOES TO WAREHAM **47**

I.
1. herself
2. maybe
3. game
4. never
5. lazy

II.
1. never, c
2. herself, e
3. lazy, a
4. game, d
5. maybe, b

18 THE BIG DAY! **53**

I.
1. garden
2. hurry
3. you're
4. sky
5. an

II.
1. NO
2. NO
3. YES
4. NO
5. YES

19 MORE RAIN FOR REBECCA **59**

I.
1. most
2. six
3. why
4. any
5. soft

II.

M	I	P	R	Q	L	W	S
A	B	A	N	Y	C	T	O
W	C	D	R	L	R	S	F
M	G	M	Q	H	I	J	T
I	K	E	W	M	O	S	T
S	I	O	F	K	M	C	S
I	J	P	W	H	Y	D	A
X	H	N	B	A	F	G	T

VOCABULARY CHECK ANSWER KEY

Lessons CTR A-11 to CTR A-20

LESSON
NUMBER

PAGE
NUMBER

20   A NEW HOME FOR REBECCA   65

I.   1. grand   II.   1. d
     2. does   2. e
     3. ago   3. a
     4. act   4. b
     5. sorry   5. c

PRONUNCIATION KEY

The pronunciation of each word is shown just after the word, in this way:
ab bre vi ate (ə brē′ vē āt).

The letters and signs used are pronounced as in the words below.

The mark ′ is placed after a syllable with primary or heavy accent, as in the example above.

The mark ´ after a syllable shows a secondary or lighter accent, as in:
ab bre vi a tion (ə brē′ vē ā′ shən).

a	hat, cap	j	jam, enjoy			t	tell, it
ā	age, face	k	kind, seek			th	thin, both
ä	father, far	l	land, coal			ŦH	then, smooth
		m	me, am				
b	bad, rob	n	no, in			u	cup, butter
ch	child, much	ng	long, bring			u̇	full, put
d	did, red					ü	rule, move
e	let, best	o	hot, rock			v	very, save
ē	equal, be	ō	open, go			w	will, woman
ėr	term, learn	ô	order, all			y	young, yet
		oi	oil, voice			z	zero, breeze
		ou	house, out			zh	measure, seizure
f	fat, if					ə	represents:
g	go, bag					a	in about
h	he, how					e	in taken
		p	paper, cup			i	in pencil
		r	run, try			o	in lemon
i	it, pin	s	say, yes			u	in circus
ī	ice, five	sh	she, rush				

CLASSICS AVAILABLE IN THIS SERIES

ORDER #	TITLE	ISBN #	READING LEVEL
CTR-101B	White Fang	1-55576-045-7	1
CTR-102B	Rebecca of Sunnybrook Farm	1-55576-046-5	1
CTR-103B	Little Women	1-55576-047-3	1
CTR-104B	Swiss Family Robinson	1-55576-049-X	1
CTR-105B	Adventures of Huckleberry Finn	1-55576-088-0	1
CTR-106B	Rip Van Winkle	1-55576-095-3	1
CTR-107B	Heidi	1-55576-178-X	1
CTR-108B	Uncle Tom's Cabin	1-55576-323-5	1
CTR-201B	Black Beauty	0-931334-51-9	2
CTR-202B	Tom Sawyer	0-931334-29-2	2
CTR-203B	The Call of the Wild	0-931334-64-0	2
CTR-204B	Treasure Island	1-55576-050-3	2
CTR-205B	The Merry Adventures of Robin Hood	1-55576-089-9	2
CTR-206B	The Prince and the Pauper	1-55576-096-1	2
CTR-207B	A Man Without a Country	1-55576-179-8	2
CTR-208B	The Hunchback of Notre Dame	1-55576-324-3	2
CTR-301B	Robinson Crusoe	0-931334-30-6	3
CTR-302B	Red Badge of Courage	0-931344-42-X	3
CTR-303B	Kidnapped	0-931334-65-9	3
CTR-304B	The Invisible Man	1-55576-063-5	3
CTR-305B	Man In the Iron Mask	1-55576-090-2	3
CTR-306B	The War of the Worlds	1-55576-097-X	3
CTR-307B	Sea Wolf	1-55576-180-1	3
CTR-308B	Oliver Twist	1-55576-325-1	3
CTR-401B	Captains Courageous	0-931334-66-7	4
CTR-402B	Dr. Jekyll & Mr. Hyde	0-931334-50-0	4
CTR-403B	Time Machine	0-931334-43-8	4
CTR-404B	Gulliver's Travels	1-55576-065-1	4
CTR-405B	20,000 Leagues Under the Sea	1-55576-091-0	4
CTR-406B	The Pathfinder	1-55576-098-8	4
CTR-407B	From the Earth to the Moon	1-55576-181-X	4
CTR-408B	David Copperfield	1-55576-322-7	4
CTR-501B	Metropolis	0-931334-68-3	5
CTR-502B	Hound of the Baskervilles	0-931344-67-5	5
CTR-503B	Kim	0-931344-69-1	5
CTR-504B	Adventures of Sherlock Holmes	1-55576-064-3	5
CTR-505B	A Journey to the Center of the Earth	1-55576-081-3	5
CTR-506B	Ivanhoe	1-55576-099-6	5
CTR-507B	Last of the Mohicans	1-55576-182-8	5
CTR-508B	Moby Dick	1-55576-326-X	5

EDCON

Long Island, New York

9 781555 760465

90000

Order No. CTR 102-11-20B
ISBN 1-55576-046-5